EMPOWERED

EMPOWERED

A Motivational Journal
for Women

MICHAELA RENEE JOHNSON, MA, LMFT

ROCKRIDGE
PRESS

For all of the people who ventured into my life—no matter how long or short of a time—and encouraged me to keep sharing and creating, and to all of the supporters who cheered me along when I hoped my words would someday inspire others globally.

This Journal Belongs to:

"

There is no limit to what we, as women, can accomplish.

"

–MICHELLE OBAMA

Introduction

I have always loved writing, especially as a way to process the depth of my emotions through difficult times. I still have my first journal, which I got in the third grade. It was included in a gift bag at a birthday party I attended. The notebook was tiny, maybe only three inches wide by four inches long, with multicolored paper and hearts on the cover. But I quickly understood that it could make a big impact on my life. It was a safe place to share my struggles with making friends at my new school and dealing with the woes of being an eight-year-old. My first journal became a friend in whom I could confide.

My journals, over the years, haven't been just a place to share frustrations and worry, but also a place where I could share dreams, especially the ones I didn't think others would understand. During challenging times, reading a great quote and writing in my journal became one of the most important ways to safely explore the change I needed, without the influence of others. My journals have always been a place where I could speak my truth and not worry about how I said it. Often, once something is written down, I feel better knowing I can let it go. And typically, I feel different about a situation once I've written about it emotionally.

I started to realize that by writing and sharing my hopes and dreams, I could even change the direction of my life. I could create positive outcomes for situations that felt overwhelming and achieve my dreams by having a safe space to journal about them.

Quickly, journaling became a tool to launch my ideas and manifest my dreams. I eventually started an online journal, which became my memoir, *Teetering on Disaster*. Writing *Empowered, A Motivational Journal for Women* is yet another dream I saw to fruition. It is a culmination of tools I've used personally to gain insight into my own needs and desires, as well as activities I've led in workshops and with my private psychotherapy clients.

Empowered is themed around the ideas of dream, believe, and achieve. In it, you'll find dozens of thought-provoking prompts, practices, and exercises to help you expand your thinking, better understand your goals, peel away the layers, discover yourself and your desires, and set the intention for your future. This journal is for anyone who has identified an area of their life that they would like to improve, whether they're looking for big changes (such as developing or realizing life goals) or minor shifts (such as tweaking the way we communicate or get our needs met).

Some exercises involve exploring your feelings and thoughts through writing, while others help you connect with your inner self through activities such as drawing, painting, or exploring nature. In creating this journal, I wanted to use creative, out-of-the-box methods to help you tap into your subconscious self. In the same way we breathe without consciously thinking about it, our subconscious mind also functions on its own, gathering data, solving problems, and creating for the future. By getting out of our comfort zones with these exercises, we can better access that inner self.

When we feel stuck, often it's because there's a building block that we need in order to move on to the next achievement. And sometimes, it may not feel comfortable. But I believe our greatest growth comes during times when we are uncomfortable—especially because humans are biologically programmed to notice when something doesn't feel right and to fix perceived problems. As you go through this journal, be aware that your mind is detecting these shifts and will help you gather insight into what needs to change. As you do the work, it is not uncommon to find yourself suddenly agitated by things that didn't bother you before or more patient in times when you typically became frustrated. You may even have alia moments or process things days later. Go easy on yourself. Don't set rules around "how" to write or "what" is okay to say.

While I've shared the idea of uncomfortable feelings arising, I also believe in the power of positive journaling to set intentions for the future and manifest our hopes, goals, and dreams. This process is about the journey, much like a river flowing to the ocean. There are smooth and rough waters, and there is beauty along the way.

For this reason, I wanted to create a space that you'll enjoy coming to, one where you'll be excited to see what unfolds—not something you feel obligated to finish. If one page doesn't align with where you are in life at the time, feel free to skip it. It may resonate better with you later, or perhaps it's simply not for you. That doesn't matter—it's more important for you to continue your journey. Conversely, if one page draws you to it over and over, that's also okay. Many of the prompts can and should be utilized more than once to gain insight surrounding the things you need, want, and can aspire to in your life.

Each exercise in this journal is derived from my own experiences, thoughts, and work as a psychotherapist and is designed to help guide and empower you to realize your true potential.

As you work through it, give yourself grace to process and practice good self-care, such as getting enough sleep, drinking plenty of water, and otherwise taking care of yourself. And remember, you are exactly where you are supposed to be in this moment. There's absolutely no right or wrong way to use this journal.

If you can connect with this journal once a week, within a year, you will have made big enough strides to begin to realize the change you want to create. If you can connect with this journal daily, you will quickly start to manifest your power to turn your dreams into reality.

Congratulations on taking the step onto this motivational journey toward achieving all that you envision for your life. Let's begin!

> Throw your dreams into space like a kite, and you do not know what it will bring back, a new life, a new friend, a new love, a new country.

–ANAÏS NIN

OUR WORLD CHANGES with the narrative we tell ourselves. We are quick to think of all the reasons that something can't or won't work out. This type of thinking can narrow the possibilities that we invite into our life. Instead, let's pretend for a moment that all the reasons why things won't work out don't exist.

What my life is now:

_____

_____

_____

_____

_____

_____

_____

What my life could be:

_____

_____

_____

_____

_____

_____

_____

"The clearer you are when visualizing your dreams, the brighter the spotlight will be to lead you on the right path."

−GAIL LYNNE GOODWIN

WHAT WE ENVISION becomes what we have. Have you ever noticed that when you are considering getting a new car, you start to see that model of car everywhere? The same is true for our goals. When we start to visualize them, our actions subconsciously move us in the direction of our dream. Create a vision board on these pages. Find pictures of things you want in your life, such as a beach vacation. Place pictures related to love on the left side (left is our heart-connection side). Don't use too many words or numbers. The space between the photos impacts when your dreams come to fruition.

"The most difficult thing is the decision to act, the rest is merely tenacity."

–AMELIA EARHART

A CLUTTERED SPACE creates a cluttered mind that can prevent us from envisioning and acting upon what we truly desire in life. Make a "spa space" in your home. Find a quiet area and incorporate relaxing elements such as a candle or a diffuser with essential oils. Put on some calming music, sit or lie comfortably, and close your eyes. Feel the comfort of knowing you are supported by the Earth, by gravity. Allow the music to completely fill your ears. Picture yourself after you have achieved your goals. What does your world look like if your dreams have come true? Stay in this space as long as you need to in order to truly envision everything you want. Write about your experience. Come to this "spa space" as often as you need to work through this journal.

"IF YOU LOOK AT WHAT YOU HAVE IN LIFE, YOU'LL HAVE MORE. IF YOU LOOK AT WHAT YOU DON'T HAVE IN LIFE, YOU'LL NEVER HAVE ENOUGH."

–OPRAH WINFREY

IT'S EASY TO FEEL overwhelmed with life as it is. This can prevent us from thinking about the future and setting goals. Consider the things that are going well in your life now and record them on the next page. Start with the simple things and expand from there.

"
Doubt is a killer. You just have to know who you are and what you stand for.

"

–JENNIFER LOPEZ

WHEN YOU THINK about the future, what hopes come to mind? Often, we focus on things we are unhappy with in life, rather than things we want to manifest. A slight shift in the way we look at the future can create space for things we never thought possible. Begin with a larger goal for the future, such as financial freedom. Then, narrow it down, focusing on something specific that you really want. Is it extra money to travel? A new place to call home?

My hopes are . . .

"I can do things you cannot, you can do things I cannot; together we can do great things."

–MOTHER TERESA

WE DON'T have to achieve our dreams entirely on our own. Who are the people in your life who offer you support and encourage you? Who are the people you can reach out to for assistance in achieving your dreams? Who can you share your dreams with? Write each of their names and why they are an integral part of your "dream team."

> "In every single thing you do, you are choosing a direction. Your life is a product of choices."

–DR. KATHLEEN HALL

OPPORTUNITY surrounds you all the time. You may not notice it because it presents itself in different ways. As you go about your week, carry this journal and write down the instances when you have a choice to make. It can be as simple as deciding whether to stop at the grocery store, head to a yoga class, or go straight home after work. For each choice you make, consider the outcome if you had chosen something else. As you start to realize the power in making choices, you can tackle them from a place of intention, moving toward achieving a goal and being mindful of that which is not serving your goals. How do your choices affect your mind-set?

_____

_____

_____

_____

_____

_____

_____

_____

"I'D RATHER REGRET THE THINGS I'VE DONE THAN REGRET THE THINGS I HAVEN'T DONE."

–LUCILLE BALL

IT'S EASY to classify ourselves by our job title or our roles in other people's lives (mom, sister) rather than see ourselves as unique people who can act on our own dreams, goals, and desires. Below, list things you've done that people might not expect—for example, that you've swung from a trapeze or that you've done karaoke. What did you feel during those experiences (strength, bravery)? Pick one of those words that resonates most with you. On the next page, write the word in large lettering, color it in, and draw around it.

_____

_____

_____

_____

_____

"

What makes you different or weird, that's your strength.

"

—MERYL STREEP

WHAT PEOPLE THINK of us and who we really are don't always match. On the next page, trace your hand. On the left side, write things most people know about you. On the right side, fill in things most people don't realize about you—things that you love about yourself and that truly make you different.

"If you are successful, it is because somewhere, sometime, someone gave you a life or an idea that started you in the right direction."

—MELINDA GATES

ALL IT TAKES is one small action to change your trajectory in life. Make a dot on the bottom left side of the next page, and label it "Today." Draw a straight line from the dot across the bottom of the page. This is the path you are currently on, without making any changes in your life. Then, make a small dot near the top of the right side of the page, and label it "Goal." Draw a diagonal line to connect it with the dot on the bottom left. On either side of the line connecting the two dots, list some actions you can take to achieve your dreams.

"Don't let anyone rob you of your imagination, your creativity, or your curiosity. It's your place in the world; it's your life."

–DR. MAE JEMISON

NO MATTER WHO YOU ARE, you have at least one skill, one thing that you are incredibly good at. If a zombie apocalypse were to happen tomorrow, and the financial system as we know it were destroyed, this skill would be your bartering tool. What is it? Do you use this skill now? Why or why not?

"ABOVE ALL, BE THE HEROINE IN YOUR LIFE, NOT THE VICTIM."

—NORA EPHRON

WE ALL HAVE an inner heroine, a part of us that can rise to the challenge in the face of adversity or emergency. Think about your heroine, your superhero self, and imagine what her armor looks like. What would her superpower be? Draw a picture of your heroine's talents.

"

Without leaps of imagination, or dreaming, we lose the excitement of possibilities. Dreaming, after all, is a form of planning.

"

–GLORIA STEINEM

IMAGINE THAT there are no limitations in your life. Imagine that all your dreams and hopes will come true in five years. Now, imagine that you are in line at your favorite coffee shop five years from now. You bump into an old friend there, and she asks, "What's new in your life? What do you have going on?" Share that story here.

"I am no bird; and no net ensnares me; I am a free human being with an independent will."

–CHARLOTTE BRONTË

SOMETIMES, our adult minds hold us back from living freely, convincing us that the things we love most are silly, embarrassing, or unimportant. Find a song you love to sing and dance to. Perhaps it's an oldie-but-goodie, or maybe it's funk, hip-hop, or glam metal. Download that song. Find some alone time in a space all your own, such as your bedroom or yard. Crank up the song and sing, dance, be wild. Share your experience. How does your adult mind hold you back from feeling free?

"Far away there in the sunshine are my highest aspirations. I may not reach them, but I can look up and see their beauty, believe in them, and try to follow where they lead."

—LOUISA MAY ALCOTT

THE NATURAL WORLD can often help connect us to our deepest thoughts and feelings. Take a walk in nature. If you live in a city, find a nearby park. Be mindful of your surroundings as you venture through nature: the foliage, the temperature, the color of the sky, the scents, the way the wildlife reacts to you. Find a comfortable space to sit, and take a few deep breaths in and out through the nose. Ask yourself, "What brings me joy?" Describe your experience.

_____

_____

_____

_____

_____

"THE DREAM IS NOT THE DESTINATION BUT THE JOURNEY."

–DIANE SAWYER

ACHIEVING DREAMS requires patience. Think of times in your life when you have been impatient and jot them down on the left page. Now, consider opportunities in your daily life to practice patience (such as at a stoplight). On the right page, share some affirmations you can say to yourself during times of impatience.

"

**Buckle up and know
that it's going to be a
tremendous amount of
work, but embrace it.**

"

–TORY BURCH

FIND A RECIPE for a dish that is delectable but a bit labor-intensive to make. Gather the ingredients. Systematically make the recipe, mindfully following each step. When you have finished baking or cooking, sit down to enjoy what you made. Take time to truly notice the smell, the flavors on your palate. Why did you choose this recipe? How did it feel upon completing each step of the process? How is making this recipe analogous with the dreams you have? How did it feel to sit and enjoy what you created?

"Often, we don't even realize who we're meant to be because we're so busy trying to live out someone else's ideas. But other people and their opinions hold no power in defining our destiny."

–OPRAH WINFREY

SOMETIMES, WE DON'T SEE our dreams to completion because someone else doesn't approve of them. You are in the driver's seat of your life, and you are responsible for creating your future. It takes courage and strength to believe in yourself in such a way that other people's opinions will not prevent you from obtaining your dreams—but you have more courage than you might think. Write about a time when you accomplished something that took immense courage.

> "Ideas bubble differently
> when we're forced to inquire
> about the obvious."

–SARA GENN

HAVE YOU EVER blown bubbles and watched as they floated away? What if our dreams and intentions were bubbles that could float to the future? Consider that each bubble is its own unique dream or intention—the minute it is thought, it is created. There is power in the idea that our intentions take shape the minute they are created. Get a jar of bubbles. Find a peaceful space to sit outside. Dip the blow tool and blow bubbles out to the universe. Imagine that each bubble is a dream that you have set on its way to happening. Write about your experience.

_____

_____

_____

_____

_____

_____

_____

"THE DREAM WAS ALWAYS RUNNING AHEAD OF ME. TO CATCH UP, TO LIVE FOR A MOMENT IN UNISON WITH IT, THAT WAS THE MIRACLE."

—ANAÏS NIN

DREAMS are often something we feel we are chasing and fighting for. But what if we view our dream as a part of the process rather than the prize we are fighting for? Then our dreams become experiences and learning opportunities that we welcome into our lives for growth. It's important to remember that everything happening now is part of the journey, and you're on your way to the top. What things are happening in your life right now that you are learning from? Dig deep and expand upon everything you are learning.

I've dreamt in my life dreams that have stayed with me ever after and changed my ideas: they've gone through and through me, like wine through water, and altered the color of my mind.

–EMILY BRONTË

OUR DREAMS don't exist on their own; each is part of a whole. Buy several shades of food coloring. Consider all the dreams you have written about thus far. One by one, state each dream and put a drop of food coloring in a bowl of water. Notice how the colors blend together on the edges, creating a new color. How will your dreams connect, mingle, and lead to other adventures? How do they build on top of one another? Write about your experience of watching the fluidity.

> "Every great dream begins with a dreamer. Always remember, you have within you the strength, the patience, and the passion to reach for the stars to change the world."

—HARRIET TUBMAN

IT'S EASY TO FEEL that our dreams are far away. And sometimes, it's difficult to remember that much of what we have now was once a dream (a driver's license, a house, a child, a certain job). Think back on times in your life when your dreams existed only in your mind. What were they? How did you achieve them?

_____

_____

_____

_____

_____

_____

_____

"Every thought we think
is creating our future."

–LOUISE HAY

AFFIRMATIONS AND MANTRAS are positive words and powerful statements about ourselves and what we can achieve (e.g., "I am" or "I can"). In large or block letters, write a few positive affirmations or mantras about yourself on these pages. Color them in.

"ONE LIFE IS ALL WE HAVE, AND WE LIVE IT AS WE BELIEVE IN LIVING IT. BUT TO SACRIFICE WHAT YOU ARE AND TO LIVE WITHOUT BELIEF, THAT IS A FATE MORE TERRIBLE THAN DYING."

–JOAN OF ARC

FOR THE EXERCISE on pages 28 and 29, you created a make-believe story in order to visualize your dreams. When we allow our limitless creation to flow, our subconscious mind begins to send messages forward to our conscious mind that help guide our actions. (This is one of the reasons creating art is so helpful for wellness and motivation.) Look for themes in your story, such as adventure or peace. Jot these themes down and elaborate on their significance in your life. These are important elements that you need in order to realize your dreams.

To dream is to have a chest filled with stars, a mind captivated by possibilities, and a heart enveloped in imagination.

—ANASTASIA BOLINDER

IT'S EASY FOR THOSE around us to sway our dreams and for us to lose sight of them. That's why we have to practice keeping them in our view. Find a constellation in the night sky. If you can see only one star, it is equally powerful. Send your wish to the constellation or star. Each night when you see it, know that it is holding space for your dreams. (It helps to do this activity during the new moon, as that's the easiest time to see stars as well as a great time for the rebirth of dreams.) On the next page, draw your constellation or star, and write your dreams within it.

"There is no greater agony than bearing an untold story inside you."

–MAYA ANGELOU

SOMETIMES, we make decisions because we think it will ensure someone is happy with us or that we will fit in. We start to believe that this is the only acceptable version of ourselves, and it begins to silence our dreams and hopes. We have an obligation to speak our truth with grace in order to live an authentic life and achieve our heart's desires. Who are you inside? What is your inner truth?

"That is your legacy on this Earth when you leave this Earth: how many hearts you touched."

–PATTI DAVIS

IT'S EASY TO GET STUCK in the idea that we aren't able to make positive change. It's easy to feel stuck against the passing of time. But the truth is, we are endless, as we are remembered by the people we touch. Each of us has the ability to change our legacy, starting with today. Whom have you touched lately and how? Whom would you like to touch positively today and in the future? Elaborate on how you will do so.

_____

_____

_____

_____

_____

_____

_____

_____

"I WILL FIGHT FOR MY
CHILDREN ON ANY LEVEL
SO THEY CAN REACH THEIR
POTENTIAL AS HUMAN BEINGS
AND IN THEIR PUBLIC DUTIES."

—DIANA, PRINCESS OF WALES

ALL OF THE STRENGTH you need lives within you already. Just as a lioness instinctively protects her den, you are capable of defending the things you want and, even more importantly, the things you need. What in your life do you need to defend and protect? How have you demonstrated strength in the past?

It's the messy parts that make us human, so we should embrace them, too—pat ourselves on the back for getting through them, rather than being angry for having gotten into them in the first place.

–JENNIFER LOPEZ

WHEN WE MAKE A MESS, we might react with shame or embarrassment. But sometimes, making a mess of one thing ends up making space for something else that is beautiful. Have you ever seen a garden in winter? The soil is muddy, and the weeds and plants are dying. After a bit of work in spring, the garden will bloom and produce a bountiful harvest in summer and fall. What messes have you made that actually made room for something lovely in the future? Elaborate on your vision.

"The only limit to the height of your achievements is the reach of your dreams and your willingness to work hard for them."

–MICHELLE OBAMA

ASK YOURSELF:

What do I want to create?

_____

_____

_____

_____

What do I want more of in my life?

_____

_____

_____

_____

What do I want to do for myself?

_____

_____

_____

_____

_____

_____

_____

_____

_____

_____

_____

_____

_____

_____

_____

_____

Get a seed packet, soil, and a pot, and plant a seed. Continue to water and fertilize your seed. Note how it grows with your attention (or doesn't, if you neglect it).

> "Owning our story can be hard, but not nearly as difficult as spending our lives running from it."

—BRENÉ BROWN

WHEN THINGS ARE MOVING along comfortably, we may not feel inspired to change. But beautiful things can grow from our most difficult times—things that wouldn't have otherwise been able to. For example, if the roof didn't leak, you may not have replaced the floor with a tile you love. When we reflect on the past, we do so with the insight of today. Reflect on difficult times. How did you heal? How did you find peace?

_____

_____

_____

_____

_____

_____

_____

_____

"REACH HIGH, FOR STARS LIE HIDDEN IN YOUR SOUL. DREAM DEEP, FOR EVERY DREAM PRECEDES THE GOAL."

–PAMELA VAULL STARR

THINK BACK TO when you were a child, or if you have children, take a few moments to observe them at play. Children believe they can build a homemade rocket ship or fly. They use their imaginations to create stories without getting into a lot of details about the how and why. It's fun to simply pretend. Tell a story with you as the main character. Where would you go? What could you do? Don't get caught up in the details.

Example: I walked out to my backyard, and there was a little boat. In the boat was a message in a bottle. It said, "Pick up the oar and row. Magic is waiting . . ."

> ## No one can feel more gratefully the charm of noble scenery or the refreshment of escape into the unspoiled solitudes of nature than the laborer at some close indoor employment.

–LUCY LARCOM

FIND A PHOTO in a magazine of a beautiful outdoor place. This should be a space that makes you feel safe, warm, and peaceful. Cut it out and paste it on the next page. Write about what draws you to this image. What about it feels safe? How does it generate feelings of peace?

"I love fantasy; I love imagination. That's the inner child in me."

–HANNAH JOHN-KAMEN

OUR INNER CHILD–the free-spirited, trusting, unjaded, imaginative version of ourselves–still exists. Find a stuffed animal, either at a store or at home, and squeeze it. Hold it tightly. Look the stuffed animal in the eyes and share your dreams with it. Give the stuffed animal a hug and thank it for listening. What was this experience like for you? If you felt uncomfortable or shy, there is an opportunity to explore why you have difficulty connecting with your inner child. Journal your thoughts.

_____

_____

_____

_____

_____

_____

_____

_____

_____

_____

_____

_____

"Always remember that you are absolutely unique. Just like everyone else."

–MARGARET MEAD

EACH SNOWFLAKE is unique and different. No two are alike. Draw a hexagon on the left page. Draw a vertical line from the top point to the bottom point of the hexagon. Draw diagonal lines connecting the other points with their opposite points. On top of the hexagon, write your nickname(s). On each line within the hexagon, write things that make you distinctive. In looking at your unique self—your snowflake—describe what you love below. What do you wish to improve upon? What would you like to add to your snowflake?

_____

_____

_____

_____

_____

_____

_____

_____

_____

_____

_____

_____

_____

"I THINK YOUR VALUES ARE ALWAYS INFLUENCED BY YOUR FAMILY AND YOUR COMMUNITY."

–DOLLY PARTON

DRAW AN OAK TREE on the next page. Begin by drawing the trunk. Extend at least five roots into the soil. Then draw branches. The trunk represents you. Write your name on it. The roots represent your values (e.g., loyalty, honesty, optimism). List them on the roots. The branches represent "I" statements to help you align with your values (e.g., "I find the good in situations"). List them on the branches. Draw grass around your tree. In the grass, list some things your tree needs to grow stronger. Below, write about the actions or things you need to practice in your life to align with your values.

_____

_____

_____

_____

_____

_____

_____

The future belongs to those who believe in the beauty of their dreams.

—ELEANOR ROOSEVELT

AS WE AGE, we lose touch with the wild and ambitious dreams we had as young children. Reflect on when you were younger, before you chose a singular career, before you became a parent or a spouse. What were some of the things you loved to do? What were some of the things you wanted to be in your life? What were your hopes? How do any of them align with the life you are leading today? Can you incorporate any of them now?

"Should you shield the canyons from the windstorms, you would never see the true beauty of their carvings."

–ELISABETH KÜBLER-ROSS

FIND A SPOT in the sun and feel the warmth of the light on your face and body. It helps you grow. On the left page, draw a picture of a large sunflower, detailing the seeds inside the head. In each seed, write your hopes, values, or wishes. On the right page, draw a picture of a windmill. Visualize the wind blowing the seeds to new heights, new places to grow.

> "The beauty of a woman must be seen from in her eyes because that is the doorway to her heart, the place where love resides."

–AUDREY HEPBURN

DRAW A PICTURE of your body on the next page. Write words within your drawing to describe what your body says to you. What does your heart tell you? Your shoulders? Your brain? Below, describe how you feel about the words your body says to you.

_____

_____

_____

_____

_____

_____

_____

_____

_____

_____

"DREAMS ARE ILLUSTRATIONS
FROM THE BOOK YOUR SOUL
IS WRITING ABOUT YOU."

—MARSHA NORMAN

DRAW A BOX on the left page. Inside the box, draw something you love or a dream. It can be specific or abstract. Now, bring that something outside the box and fill the page by expanding upon your drawing, leaving no white space and including as many details as possible. On the right page, describe how it felt to be trapped by the box you created. How did it feel to be free of it?

> ## It is only in our darkest hours that we may discover the true strength of the brilliant light within ourselves that can never, ever be dimmed.

—DOE ZANTAMATA

SOMETIMES, the hardest thing about challenges is not knowing the outcome or feeling worried about the unknown. Draw a crystal ball on the top half of the next page. Consider whatever is going on in life that you are worried about. Now, imagine that your crystal ball peers into the future and sees the solution or outcome. Draw or write your outcome in the crystal ball. On the bottom half of the page, describe how it felt to think about challenging times when you knew what the outcome could be. What action can you take toward impacting the outcome?

"I have learned that as long as I hold fast to my beliefs and values—and follow my own moral compass—then the only expectations I need to live up to are my own."

–MICHELLE OBAMA

OUR LIVES ARE FULL of expectations from others, whether we realize them or not. Draw four columns on the top half of the next page. Label them "My Hats," "What I Give," "What I Get," and "What I'm Missing." Start with "My Hats"—all the titles and roles you feel define you (e.g., mom, friend, teacher). Then, fill in the other columns. Are there common trends? On the bottom half of the page, write about what you can let go of to create space for more of what you want. How can you detach from these expectations with love and start living up to your own?

"Follow what you are genuinely passionate about and let that guide you to your destination."

–DIANE SAWYER

SOMETIMES, in order to envision the future, you have to look to the past. List the highlights of the past year. Then, write a story about what your life will look like in the next year. Where will you go, and what will you accomplish? Be specific.

"VULNERABILITY IS THE BIRTHPLACE OF INNOVATION, CREATIVITY, AND CHANGE."

–BRENÉ BROWN

SHAMEFUL EXPERIENCES from our past often keep us from feeling comfortable with vulnerability. But embracing our vulnerability enables us to explore the things that prevent us from working toward our goals. When we believe that it's okay to dive into our goals—regardless of our fears of being judged, being hurt, or failing—we create space to accomplish more than we've ever expected. Watch Brené Brown's TED Talk, "The Power of Vulnerability." In what ways do you feel shame? In what ways are you vulnerable? Journal any other thoughts you have.

"
Optimism is the faith that leads to achievement. Nothing can be done without hope and confidence.

"

–HELEN KELLER

FLIP BACK to your affirmations or mantras on pages 48 and 49. How do you feel about them now? Would you change them or keep them the same? If you were to change them, how would you do so? Write an affirmation or mantra in large block letters on the next page and color it in.

> "The best time to plant a tree was 20 years ago. The second-best time is now."

–CHINESE PROVERB

IDEA PLUS ACTION creates result. It's beautiful to dream (big or small), and it's wonderful to believe in yourself and your goals. But the only way to achieve your dreams is through actions. Often in life, we want to make it to our destination quickly for an up-close look. But sometimes, the best perspective isn't up close. We need to step back to really take everything in. Write about how you can step back to see your dream more clearly. Include three small action steps and three big action steps.

> ## "If there is magic on this planet, it is contained in water."
>
> **—LOREN EISELEY**

WATER BY ITS NATURE holds us when we trust it and allow it to. Dreams are similar to water—if we fight them, we might sink. Find a mantra that resonates with you. Fill a bathtub or get in a pool. Take a few deep breaths and float. Try to also visualize your mantra floating. Notice when you sink or float and how your breath changes your body in the water. Once you're out, do this breathing technique: Sit straight but comfortably. Inhale deeply through your mouth. Exhale through your mouth in short, quick successive breaths until you are out of air. Breathe in deeply through your nose, exhale through your mouth in one breath. Allow your breath to return to its effort-less state. What did it feel like to force your breath out? To breathe deeply in one breath? What does your mantra look like in the written word? What does it look like in action? How can you relax in such a way that you can allow space for your mantra?

"ONE OF THE OLDEST HUMAN NEEDS IS HAVING SOMEONE TO WONDER WHERE YOU ARE WHEN YOU DON'T COME HOME AT NIGHT."

—MARGARET MEAD

IN LIFE, we have wants (fancy new car), and we have needs (well-running car that allows us to get to work). Sometimes, we can become unclear about the difference. This can create confusion when working toward our goals. On the left page, write all of your wants. On the right page, write all of your needs.

_____

_____

_____

_____

_____

_____

_____

_____

_____

_____

_____

_____

_____

_____

_____

> # Follow your dreams. If you have a goal, and you want to achieve it, then work hard, and do everything you can to get there, and one day it will come true.

–LINDSEY VONN

WITH A LARGE GOAL, it can be easy to get overwhelmed by all it will take to achieve it. It's helpful to remember that you don't have to accomplish every step today or even next month. Label the top left part of the next page "Success." Below it, write your goal (buying a house, summiting a mountain). Label the bottom right part of the page "Beginning." From there, draw a winding path to "Success." Add obstacles along the way (unexpected bills, an unpredictable training schedule). Finish by adding big and small milestones (reaching a savings goal, joining a climbing gym).

> "Worry does not empty tomorrow of its sorrow. It empties today of its strength."

–CORRIE TEN BOOM

WHEN WE RECOGNIZE the power in our thoughts and decide to do something productive with our worries, our worrying becomes intentional rather than reactive. Any time we can lead our emotions with intention, we have the ability to feel empowered. Get out a timer and set it for five minutes. For the next five minutes, worry, be angry, be sad about all the things that aren't going well in your life. List them below. Dive deeper and try to identify why these things worry you. Ask yourself if anything about these situations or problems is within your control.

"Hope is the thing with feathers. That perches in the soul. And sings the tunes without the words. And never stops at all."

–EMILY DICKINSON

ON PAGE 102, you listed things you were worried about. Write something positive or hopeful about some or all of those situations. List one action you could take to improve each one of your worries. Now, imagine that your worries or burdens are completely gone. How would your life be different? What would your life look like?

_____

_____

_____

_____

_____

_____

_____

_____

_____

_____

"YOU JUST KEEP A POSITIVE ATTITUDE NO MATTER WHAT COMES IN YOUR WAY—CHALLENGES, ROADBLOCKS. DON'T LET IT FAZE YOU, AND YOU CAN OVERCOME ANYTHING."

–ROSE NAMAJUNAS

SOMETIMES, it is important to find new ways to maneuver around obstacles you experience frequently. Dim the lights (but don't turn them off) and walk through the house as if it were an obstacle course. As you walk, consider how it feels to move around the space now, negotiating obstacles that you can easily maneuver around in the daylight. Once you complete the activity, keep the lights low, sit or lie down with your journal, and write about the experience. How did it feel? How do you approach these obstacles? How does it feel to write on this page in the dark?

I attribute my success to this: I never gave or took any excuse.

–FLORENCE NIGHTINGALE

HAVING A NO-EXCUSES APPROACH helps us take the steps toward realizing our true potential. Let's start with setting a few intentions for the coming months.

One to-do item or project I will complete: _____

_____

One book I will to read to help me achieve my dream: _____

_____

One quiet-time activity I will engage in that calms me: _____

_____

One hobby I will take up: _____

_____

One important thing I will accomplish: _____

_____

How can following through with these intentions help you realize your dream?

_____

_____

_____

_____

_____

List five things you will do to hold yourself accountable.

_____

_____

_____

_____

_____

"For me, singing sad songs often has a way of healing a situation. It gets the hurt out in the open into the light, out of the darkness."

–REBA McENTIRE

TURN OFF all the lights around you. Find a safe and comfortable space to sit. Play a sad song. Listen to it completely. Journal your thoughts. Once again, turn off all the lights, but this time play a happy song. Listen to it completely. Now, notice that in the dark room, the tiniest illumination of light can dance like hope in the darkness. Journal your thoughts.

"Self-knowledge is essential not only to writing, but to doing almost anything really well. It allows you to work through from a deep place— from the deep, dark corners of your subconscious mind."

—MEG ROSOFF

INKBLOTS CAN BE a very insightful tool for revealing our subconscious thoughts and emotions. Gather three colors of acrylic paint and a piece of plain paper. Squeeze the paint freely on the paper in any pattern you like, staying away from the edges. Be careful not to squeeze large blobs. Fold the paper in half and reopen to reveal the inkblot that has emerged. What do you see? How do you feel? How would you interpret it? Is there any message in what you created? Elaborate on your thoughts.

"WHAT I WANT FOR MY FANS AND FOR THE WORLD, FOR ANYONE WHO FEELS PAIN, IS TO LEAN INTO THAT PAIN AND EMBRACE IT AS MUCH AS THEY CAN AND BEGIN THE HEALING PROCESS."

–LADY GAGA

WHEN WE'RE IN PAIN, it can be difficult to think about our dreams or anything else. Writing about it can be a release. Write a letter to someone who has hurt you that you never intend to send. Share how they have made you feel.

Dear _____ ,

_____

_____

_____

_____

_____

_____

_____

_____

_____

_____

_____

Now, write a letter to someone who has brought you great happiness or done something kind. Write freely as if you will never send it. This will help you speak honestly, without any fear of how you sound.

*Dear*_____,

_____

_____

_____

_____

_____

_____

_____

_____

_____

_____

If your dreams do not scare you, they are not big enough.

—ELLEN JOHNSON SIRLEAF

SOMETIMES, in order to embrace your future, you have to reimagine how you view yourself or your past. On the left page, write about or draw the past in pencil. On the right page, write about or draw the future in color.

"If you fall in love with the imagination, you understand that it is a free spirit. It will go anywhere, and it can do anything."

—ALICE WALKER

ON PAGE 69, you pasted a photo of a beautiful place that made you feel safe and at peace. Glance at that photo again. Close your eyes for three to five minutes and envision yourself in that space. After you open your eyes, journal your thoughts.

> "Creative people do not see things for what they are; they see them for what they can be."

—JULIE ISRAEL

GET A PIECE OF PLAIN PAPER and gather some finger paint, selecting colors that make you feel calm. Before you begin, visualize your inner child. If it helps, visualize yourself in kindergarten. As a child, you could see an entire world from the simplest drawings on a page. You could look at fluffy clouds and see a bunny, a dragon, or any other kind of creature. Finger paint freely while visualizing your dream. On these pages, write about what it felt like to be free of limitations.

_____

_____

_____

_____

_____

_____

_____

_____

"IMAGINATION IS THE HIGHEST KITE ONE CAN FLY."

–LAUREN BACALL

IMAGINE your ideal day. How does it begin? What are the biggest highlights? How does it end? How can you make space for at least one of these things every day?

If I waited for perfection, I would never write a word.

–MARGARET ATWOOD

MORE OFTEN THAN NOT, we stick our toes in to test to the water when we're considering a new idea, action, or way of thinking. It's okay to be unsure whether you want to dive in, but while you're testing the water, you can still make progress. Think about your dreams and as many adjectives as you can to describe them. Fill the next page with those adjectives. What do those adjectives create in your life that doesn't exist now?

"I would venture to guess that Anon, who wrote so many poems without signing them, was often a woman."

–VIRGINIA WOOLF

REFLECT ON the Elizabeth Kübler-Ross quote on page 78. Consider everything it means to you, particularly as you navigate toward your dreams. Add several more lines to it here to create a poem (it's okay if it doesn't rhyme).

"I saw music as a way to entertain people and take them away from their daily lives and put smiles on their faces, as opposed to what I see it being now, which is a way for me to actually communicate, and a way for me to tap into my subconscious."

—ALANIS MORISSETTE

SYNCHRONICITIES are moments in our lives when unrelated events occur in a meaningful manner, allowing us to receive messages through them. Perhaps someone crosses your mind and then you receive a text from them. These messages are windows to opportunity, delicate combinations of something so vast and yet so intricate. Turn on the radio. Listen to the next song that comes on. What did you feel in listening to it? Were there any messages for you?

_____

_____

_____

_____

_____

_____

_____

_____

_____

_____

_____

_____

_____

_____

_____

_____

_____

"YOU ARE MORE POWERFUL THAN YOU KNOW; YOU ARE BEAUTIFUL JUST AS YOU ARE."

—MELISSA ETHERIDGE

YOU HAVE CONTROL over your emotions, though it often may not feel that way. Sometimes, it's helpful to give your subconscious a way to talk to your conscious self to better connect with your emotions. Below, write down three emotions you have been experiencing lately. Gather some colored pencils or markers and select a color for each emotion. Using only those three colors, draw a quick picture on the top half of the next page related to your current emotional state. On the bottom half of the next page, reflect on the emotions you assigned to each color. How did those emotions come out on paper? How are those emotions helping or hurting you in obtaining your dreams?

"

You can't predict it all.
People will tell you to plan
things out as best you
can. They will tell you to
focus. They will tell you
to follow your dreams.
They will all be right.

"

–ELIZABETH WARREN

SOMETIMES, we get in the way of accomplishing our own dreams. On the next page, write down the things that are serving you, the things that are not serving you, what you can control, and what you cannot control. Then, consider how you can let go of the things that are not serving you and that you cannot control in order to make space to realize your dreams.

"I'm making space for the unknown future to fill up my life with yet-to-come surprises."

–ELIZABETH GILBERT

YOU HAVE WORKED incredibly hard to look within, silence negative self-talk, identify with your power and strength, and find clarity with the true direction in which your heart is sending you. Draw a compass rose on the left page. Where cardinal north is, write, "I am…" Where east is, write, "I will…" Where west is, write, "I believe…" Where south is, write, "I can…" On page 14, you identified your dream team. Call someone from your dream team. Share and elaborate on these affirmations and your dreams with them. Below, journal about your experience.

References

Angelou, Maya. *I Know Why the Caged Bird Sings*. New York, NY: Random House, 1969.

AZQuotes. "Melissa Etheridge Quotes." Accessed January 12, 2020. azquotes.com/author/4570-Melissa_Etheridge.

BrainyQuote. "Alanis Morissette Quotes." Accessed January 12, 2020. brainyquote.com/quotes/alanis_morissette_233060.

BrainyQuote. "Alice Walker Quotes." Accessed January 12, 2020. brainyquote.com/quotes/alice_walker_625848.

BrainyQuote. "Amelia Earhart Quotes." Accessed January 12, 2020. brainyquote.com/quotes/amelia_earhart_120929.

BrainyQuote. "Anaïs Nin Quotes." Accessed January 12, 2020. brainyquote.com/quotes/anais_nin_121253.

BrainyQuote. "Audrey Hepburn Quotes." Accessed January 12, 2020. brainyquote.com/authors/audrey-hepburn-quotes.

BrainyQuote. "Corrie ten Boom Quotes." Accessed January 12, 2020. brainyquote.com/authors/corrie-ten-boom-quotes.

BrainyQuote. "Eleanor Roosevelt Quotes." Accessed January 12, 2020. brainyquote.com/quotes/eleanor_roosevelt_100940.

BrainyQuote. "Elisabeth Kübler-Ross Quotes." Accessed January 12, 2020. brainyquote.com/quotes/elisabeth_kublerross_387073.

BrainyQuote. "Elizabeth Warren Quotes." Accessed January 12, 2020. brainyquote.com/quotes/elizabeth_warren_690804.

BrainyQuote. "Florence Nightingale Quotes." Accessed January 12, 2020. brainyquote.com/quotes/florence_nightingale_391864.

BrainyQuote. "Hannah John-Kamen Quotes." Accessed January 12, 2020. brainyquote.com/quotes/hannah_johnkamen_887909.

BrainyQuote. "Jennifer Lopez Quotes." Accessed January 12, 2020. brainyquote.com/quotes/jennifer_lopez_460714.

BrainyQuote. "Joan of Arc Quotes." Accessed January 12, 2020. brainyquote.com/authors/joan-of-arc-quotes.

BrainyQuote. "Lauren Bacall Quotes." Accessed January 12, 2020. brainyquote.com/quotes/lauren_bacall_379178.

BrainyQuote. "Lindsey Vonn Quotes." Accessed January 12, 2020. brainyquote.com/authors/lindsey-vonn-quotes.

BrainyQuote. "Louisa May Alcott Quotes." Accessed January 12, 2020. brainyquote.com/quotes/louisa_may_alcott_121254.

BrainyQuote. "Louise Hay Quotes." Accessed January 12, 2020. brainyquote.com/quotes/louise_l_hay_170242.

BrainyQuote. "Lucille Ball Quotes." Accessed January 12, 2020. brainyquote.com/quotes/lucille_ball_384638.

BrainyQuote. "Margaret Atwood Quotes." Accessed January 12, 2020. brainyquote.com/authors/margaret-atwood-quotes.

BrainyQuote. "Margaret Mead Quotes." Accessed January 12, 2020. brainyquote.com/quotes/margaret_mead_141040.

BrainyQuote. "Margaret Mead Quotes." Accessed January 12, 2020. brainyquote.com/authors/margaret-mead-quotes.

BrainyQuote. "Meg Rosoff Quotes." Accessed January 12, 2020. brainyquote.com/quotes/meg_rosoff_530576.

BrainyQuote. "Patti Davis Quotes." Accessed January 12, 2020. brainyquote.com/quotes/patti_davis_671739.

BrainyQuote. "Princess Diana Quotes." Accessed January 12, 2020. brainyquote.com/search_results?q=princess+diana.

BrainyQuote. "Rose Namajunas Quotes." Accessed January 12, 2020. brainyquote.com/authors/rose-namajunas-quotes.

BrainyQuote. "Virginia Woolf Quotes." Accessed January 12, 2020. brainyquote.com/authors/virginia-woolf-quotes.

Brontë, Charlotte ("Currer Bell"). *Jane Eyre*. London, England: Smith, Elder and Co., 1847.

Brontë, Emily ("Ellis Bell"). *Wuthering Heights*. London, England: Thomas Cautley Newby, 1847.

Brown, Brené. *The Gifts of Imperfection: Let Go of Who You Think You're Supposed to Be and Embrace Who You Are*. Center City, MN: Hazelden Publishing, 2010.

Brown, Brené. "The Power of Vulnerability." TEDxHouston, 2010.

Dickinson, Emily. *Hope Is the Thing with Feathers: The Complete Poems of Emily Dickinson*. Layton, UT: Gibbs Smith Publisher, 2019.

Eiseley, Loren. *The Immense Journey: An Imaginative Naturalist Explores the Mysteries of Man and Nature*. New York, NY: Random House, 1959.

Ephron, Nora. Commencement address, Wellesley College. Wellesley, MA. 1996.

Forbes, Moira. "Billionaire Tory Burch's Seven Lessons for Entrepreneurs." Forbes. May 22, 2013.

Gallop Goodman, Gerda. *Diane Sawyer: Women of Achievement*. Broomhall, PA: Chelsea House Publishers, 2001.

Gates, Melinda. Commencement address, Ursuline Academy. Dallas, TX. 1982.

Gilbert, Elizabeth. *Eat, Pray, Love*. London, England: Penguin Books, 2006.

Gloria Steinem's Office. "News." Accessed January 12, 2020. gloriasteinem.com/news.

Goodreads. "Anastasia Bolinder > Quotes." Accessed January 12, 2020. goodreads.com/author/quotes/15903201. Anastasia_Bolinder.

Goodreads. "Chinese Proverb > Quotes." Accessed January 12, 2020. goodreads.com/author/quotes/15516098. Chinese_Proverb.

Goodreads. "Doe Zantamata > Quotes." Accessed January 12, 2020. goodreads.com/author/quotes/6031956. Doe_Zantamata.

Goodreads. "Ellen Johnson Sirleaf > Quotes." Accessed January 12, 2020. goodreads.com/author/quotes/2116089. Ellen_Johnson_Sirleaf.

Goodreads. "Harriet Tubman > Quotes." Accessed January 12, 2020. goodreads.com/author/quotes/59710.Harriet_Tubman.

Goodreads. "Jennifer Lopez > Quotes." Accessed January 12, 2020. goodreads.com/author/quotes/82052.Jennifer_Lopez.

Goodreads. "Pamela Vaull Starr > Quotes." Accessed January 12, 2020. goodreads.com/author/quotes/214632. Pamela_Vaull_Starr.

Goodwin, Gail Lynne. InspireMeToday.com. Accessed November 4, 2019. inspiremetoday.com/photos.

Hall, Kathleen. *Alter Your Life: Overbooked? Overworked? Overwhelmed?* Clarkesville, GA: Oak Haven, 2005.

Johnson, Frank. *The Wit and Wisdom of Dolly Parton*. Scotts Valley, CA: Create Space Independent Publishing, 2014.

Keller, Helen. *The Story of My Life*. New York, NY: Doubleday, Page & Company, 1905.

Larcom, Lucy. *An Idyl of Work*. Boston, MA: James R. Osgood and Company, 1875.

Nin, Anaïs. *The Diary of Anaïs Nin, Volume Four, 1944-1947*. San Diego, CA: Harcourt, Brace Jovanovich, 1971.

Norman, Marsha. *The Fortune Teller*. New York, NY: Random House, 1987.

Oprah.com. "Defining Destiny: What I Know for Sure." Accessed January 12, 2020. oprah.com/omagazine/what-oprah -knows-for-sure-about-destiny.

PassItOn. "Julie Israel." Accessed January 12, 2020. passiton.com /search?q=julie+israel.

QuoteFancy. "Diane Sawyer Quotes." Accessed January 12, 2020. quotefancy.com/diane-sawyer-quotes.

QuoteFancy. "Mae Jemison Quotes." Accessed January 12, 2020. quotefancy.com/mae-jemison-quotes.

QuoteFancy. "Mother Teresa Quotes." Accessed January 12, 2020. quotefancy.com/mother-teresa-quotes.

QuoteFancy. "Sara Genn Quotes." Accessed January 12, 2020. quotefancy.com/sara-genn-quotes.

Quotes. "Oprah Winfrey Quotes." Accessed January 12, 2020. quotes.net/quote/19128.

Streep, Meryl. Honorary degree acceptance speech, Indiana University. Bloomington, IN. April 16, 2014.

Stubbs, Dan. "Lady Gaga – The Full NME Cover Interview." NME. October 21, 2016. nme.com/features/lady-gaga-full-nme -cover-interview-1672409.

The White House, President Barack Obama. "Remarks by the First Lady at Tuskegee University Commencement Address." May 9, 2015.

Acknowledgments

I'd like to thank Callisto Media for giving me the opportunity to create and encouraging me to make this journal the best it could be. Lori Tenny, thank you for seeing the potential in the activities and helping me expand on so many of them. I'm proud of what we accomplished. I'd also like to thank my family for always holding the belief that I can see my dreams shape into reality. Lastly, a big thanks to my husband and son, whose perspectives on life help me grow into a better version of myself daily, reminding me to always save space for gratitude and help me reconnect with what's most important to me.

About the Author

Michaela Renee Johnson, MA, LMFT, is an award-winning author, licensed psycho-therapist, and host of the top iTunes podcast *Be You Find Happy*, which encourages people to speak their truth with grace and live a courageous life of authenticity. Through her Be You Find Happy initiative, she also holds workshops and conversations on finding happiness in spite of life's setbacks, and she speaks on the topic of happiness across the nation. She is an avid adventurer, having traveled to more than 20 countries, and is a self-proclaimed "Boho Mom" who loves all things metaphysical as well as poetic quotes. She is a Sagittarius and an ocean lover who lives in Northern California with her husband, young son, and a homestead full of animals. In her spare time, she is often hiking, doing yoga, gardening, golfing, or reading. Connect with her online at MichaelaRenee.com and on Instagram @michaelareneej.